RHAPSODIES 1831

Rhapsodies 1831

PETRUS BOREL

TRANSLATED FROM
THE FRENCH
BY JOHN GALLAS
AND KURT GÄNZL

CARCANET POETRY

First published in Great Britain in 2022 by
Carcanet Press Ltd
Alliance House, 30 Cross Street
Manchester M2 7AQ
www.carcanet.co.uk

A CIP catalogue record for this book is
available from the British Library.

ISBN 978 1 80017 220 3

Book design by Andrew Latimer
Printed in Great Britain by SRP Ltd, Exeter, Devon

The publisher acknowledges financial
assistance from Arts Council England.

CONTENTS

Petrus Borel (1809–59) was born in Lyons, the twelfth of fourteen children. His early education rendered him atheistic and anti-clerical, solitary, erudite, pedantic and self-dramatizing, with a passion for things Mediaeval. He abandoned his Architectural profession and entered the Romantic Movement, and *Le Petit Cénacle*, a Parisian, anti-Classicist, revolutionary and Republican band of *bizarristes* who dressed, spoke, partied, wrote and posed in Freedom. The group included Théophile Gautier, Jehan de Seigneur, Eugène Devéria, Joseph Bouchardy and Gérard de Nerval. Disappointed by the July Revolution of 1830 ('I do need a *vast* amount of Liberty'), Borel and his friends buried themselves for a time in grotesqueries, the macabre, carnivals, Dandyism, and considered outlandish behaviour ('Les Bouzingos').

Petrus Borel published *Rhapsodies,* here presented in its entirety, in 1831. He thought it a book that 'wrote itself', filled with suffering, bitterness, revolution, and what Borel called the 'slag of hot-metal refining'. Enid Starkie, however, the author of the only relatively modern biography of Borel (1954) considers the poems 'mostly gentle and sentimental'. 'There are in *Rhapsodies* however poems which give Borel the right to an individual and permanent place in French poetry.' The book was an intense influence on Baudelaire. But its publication created no stir.

Borel went on to write 'gothicky' short stories, the scandalous 'Madame Putiphar' (1838), became a journalist and magazine-writer, and, declining in belief and remuneration, went to Algeria as a Civil Servant, where he (according to sources) did, or decidedly did not, do the administration work that was expected of him. He died in Algeria after being removed from his post and digging too long in his garden without a hat. 'Everything God does He does well, and would have left me my hair if He intended to protect me'. There is no known grave.

The sobriquet 'The Lycanthrope', now universally applied to references to Borel, and the subtitle of Starkie's biography, was originally simply Borel's own opinion of his powers and desire to attack conventional society, tyrants, Classicism, traditionalism etc. Borel wrote a short story entitled 'Champavert le Lycanthrope', professedly autobiographical, in his collection *Immoral Tales* (1838). The wild seductions, knifings, general bloodshed, sadism, sexual shenanigans, corpses, dissections etc. in these stories have subsumed the nickname into something simply creepy. His portrait, thin, darkly besuited, his right hand on the head of a great hound, helps.

*

These poems were translated by the method used for *The Song Atlas* and *52 Euros* (both Carcanet anthologies): a native speaker, in this case my brother Kurt Gänzl, translated each word, line, verse and poem into meticulous and practical English; I then 're-poemed' them. I have no beliefs, or even opinions, on the matter of translation, its theory or practise: if a poet gives his/her all to a translation, it will be rather like that poet's own work. It is better that a reader gets my full-throttled versions of Petrus Borel than a hesitant attempt to copy rhyme, rhythm, structure or contemporary contexts, which will, and cannot help but, lower the percentage of drive.

For the life of Petrus Borel there is really only, in English, *Petrus Borel: the Lycanthrope* by Dame Enid Starkie (Faber and Faber, 1954). The French text of *Rhapsodies* can be read in Wikisource.

> *'Proud, splendid, brave – my dear adviser,*
> *Whose stubborn heart collides with what he loves'*
> – Henri de Régnier

> *'To ye who Critic everything,*
> *to ye who mock and scoff,*
> *this little book of verse I bring –*
> *so, merci, bugger off!'*
> – François de Malherbe

A child must burble before it speaks with common ease: a poet must burble also, and I have dribbled after my fashion –
Behold!
The metal that boils in the crucible must fling forth its slag: the poetry that boils in my heart has slung its dross –
Behold!
Are then these Rhapsodies mere spittle and drool?
Indeed.
And why, knowing this, do I seek to please the public? Why do I not shut up, and quietly fade away?
Because I wish to part with these poems forever: I wish to appear as I am: I wish to hang them upon a wall, and turn away, for as long as I keep them close, so long will I return to look at them again. Now I shall give them away; for a new stage of life begins for the poet only after he has revealed his work and himself, and the long occupation of the heights is done. A painter needs his Show; a poet needs his Publication.
If you read my book, you shall know me. Poor it may be; and so I truly am. I have not written merely to write. There is no disguise. I do not dissemble. It is a collection of coincidence,

where cries of pain and cries of joy are cast amidst a childhood rarely wasted, often tortuous, and always poor.

If these verses should seem obvious and ordinary, rarely touching the kingdom of heaven, then you may blame my position in life, which has had nothing heavenly about it.

Reality ever lends me its hand, poverty ever keeps my feet upon the earth whenever I am inclined toward the enthusiasms of higher flights.

I am neither a cynic nor a prude: to drag from me some breast-beaten poem, my wound must be great: I am never merely the moaning patient stricken with consumption.

If I seem to have enjoyed showing off my poverty, it is because I am nauseated by our poets of the present age, whose so-called verse, whose barbarous luxury, whose aristocratic bent, whose ecclesiastical flummeries and sonnets-in-chains are like listening to hair-shirted hacks bum-branded with their armorials, clutching a rosary or a rattle in their fists.

Behold the stuck-up daughters of their dreams, their Countesses... their Duchesses!... rather their washerwomen!

If I have remained apart from them, obscure and unknown; if no one has ever beaten the drum for me; if I have never been called 'The Eagle!' or 'The Swan!' – then, upon the other hand, I have never played the puppet or the clown, or called a crowd to me to hear me as a Master with beating on a tambourine. And no man may say that I have been his apprentice.

Of course, the bourgeoisie will not be alarmed by the names of those to whom I dedicate the poems of this volume: they are simply young men like myself, men with heart and courage whom I grew up with, and whom I love entirely!

It is they who banish from my thoughts the dullness of life. They are honest all, friends, comrades of brotherhoods and tight-knit bands – not the paste-boarded gaggle of M. Henri delaTouche... who could never understand. Should I desist from advancing our humble names amongst great men? We are Titian and Ariosto, Molière and Mignard.

To these, my sweet companions, I give this book! It was written amongst you, and you may claim it as your own.

It is for you, Jehan Duseigneur, Sculptor, fair and kindly, faithful and inexhaustible in work, yet artless as a girl. Take heart! You will have your lasting day and France will have a sculptor of Her own at last –

It is for you, Napoléon Thom, Painter, the hand, honour, cast of a soldier! Take heart! The breath of genius is yours! –

It is for you, dear Gérard! When shall the Arbiters of Art admit upon the public the pictures that they huddle over at their little parties? –

It is for you, Vigneron, who owns my deepest friendship, who proves to those of fainter hearts what perseverance may accomplish; and Jasmerai Duval, like a student-puppy, fed well at your bowl. –

It is for you, Joseph Bouchardy, Engraver, heart of gunpowder! –

For you, Théophile Gautier! – For you, Alphonse Brot! – For you, Augustus Mac-Keat! – For you, Vabre! For you, Léon! For you, O'Neddy! For all who I love!

You who judge me by this book, and find me wanting, will be mistaken; those who crown me with laurels will be mistaken. This is no pose of small humility. For you who would accuse me of duncical nonsense – I have my poet's faith, and laugh at you.

I have no more to say, except that I might very well have made this Preface a paranymphian éthopée, or an extended Thesis *ex professa* – but would it not be ridiculous to put my Preface up for sale, and say so much about so little?

Also, some poems are dipped in Politics. Shall I be put to scorn and anathemized as a Republican? Well, I am one. Let that prepare you.

Ask the old Duke of Orleans if he recalls a voice that pursued him when he took the Oath within the Chamber on the 9th of August, throwing in his face the shouts of Liberty! and the Republic! amidst the acclamations of his rented crowd?

Yes, I am a Republican, but it is not July's fine sun that has made of such ideals a sudden blossom! I have been so since childhood. Ah, not a Republican dancing with red or blue stockings, some barn-orator or planter of Poplars! I am a Republican in the way of the lynx: I am a Republican in the way of the wolf!

If I speak of a Republic it is because the word, to me, represents the greatest liberty that can be achieved by Society and Civilisation. I am a Republican because I could not be a Caribbeanist; I require a quite enormous amount of Freedom: shall the Republic give me this? I have yet to be so blessed.

But when this hope is disappointed, I shall still, like many others, have my *Missouri*. When I am there, ravaged as I am, embittered by so much misfortune, I may dream of Equality, I may come here to the Consitution of the Countryside, which surpasses the approbation of mere men.

To those who shall say that this volume is the work of a lunatic, of some Romantic Mountain-Goat who thrusts 'Souls' and 'Dear God' into fashion, who, according to the *Figaro*, dines on babies and makes moonshine in skulls – you I can avoid. I have your description:

frowning brow; forcep-strangled expression; ropey hair; strap of bristly crackling upon each side of the face; extensive shirt-collar like a double-triangulated sheet; stovepipe hat; umbrella.

To those who shall say that this volume is the work of a Saint-Simoniac!... to those who say it is the work of a Republican, a King-Eater: he must be done to Death!... Well, they will be the little shopkeepers who have no customers: the disappointed grocer is a tiger!... the State Officials who might lose all upon the change of the wind: the State Official is a Phillppist, a pompom-maker!

These are good people all, these guillotine-and-paper-money-Republicans, these Head-Dispensers – who do not understand the high enterprise of Saint-Just, but reproach him for his necessary severities, and yet heap praise upon the carnages of Buonaparte! and Buonaparte's eight million dead!

To those who shall say that this book is surbuban and distasteful, my answer is that mockery never made the Best Bed: is this work not all fitting for an age, which has for its government ignorant Accountants and Gun-Traders, and has for its King a man whose battle-cry is 'Praise God and my Shops!'?

Happily, to console us for such things, we have still Adultery! Maryland tobacco! and those little rolling-papers from Spain to make our cigarillos with.

PROLOGUE

to Léon Clopet, architect

'Behold, I will do a new thing. Now it shall spring forth. And the beasts of the field shall honour me, the dragons and the owls'
– Bible

When your Petrus, or Pierre,
had no stone to make his chair,
no more sighs or tears to shed,
and ne'er a nail above his bed
to hang his old guitar upon,
you gave me shelter, dear Léon.

Come, little Rhapsodist, you said,
write your poems, eat my bread,
although the sky is hardly blue
and Homer's heav'n is not for you,
nor that which warmed the troubadour,
for here 'tis cold, and you are poor.

Ah, Paris has no forest free,
so come, my little poet, to me,
where pinched but happy we may live
and friendship to each other give.
And we will share our little lot
of sweet hashish till all's forgot!

My humble and ashamed soul
thus blessed the friend that made it whole
and helped it in its misery.
For in my cruel adversity,
struck long and low with anxious fear,
you only, Léon, shed a tear!

Do not naysay my gratitude:
should I naysay your fire and food?
I cannot hide my thanks to thee –
ah, no, my dear Protector, see,
I tell the world my dire distress,
uncovered in my nakedness!

And wish it that the world may know
I did not flinch; for I can show
two lots of earthly pain, at least,
at this, the world's all-sumptuous feast!
For poverty ne'er broke my youth,
or cracked the brittle branch of truth.

And wish it that the world may see
my beard is not the all of me!
I have my heart, I have my song,
that smile when troubles come along.
I have my guiding soul, whose fee
is unretreating victory!

And wish the world may understand
that with no buckler in my hand,
no Lordship or no Kingly place,
no Gentleman's too-flattering face,
no Usurer's ill-gotten gains –
I am no Byron for my pains.

I write no elegies for Courts
amidst their lusts and wastrel sports,
no hymns to Gods do I rehearse,
no lady's thigh displays my verse
that springs from wealth and gluttony:
my song is of my poverty.

BENONI
lament for my brother

His youth, not always kept from need,
touched him with gall, and a wary nerve,
wreckage, sure, of Want's old beggary
broke against Freedom
dunned by a richer mind:
that finished me!

Now he sleeps, my Benoni, and suffers the less,
the first sweet quiet supped for an age.
He has slept one whole day since his eyes milked over
and he pressed my hand in his feebled own
and said, 'You all love me: now let it come!'
He is sleeping, my Benoni.

He is sleeping, my Benoni: come,
tiptoe and see him becalmed; hush, hush,
make no sound to rewake him,
come quietly here in the private Best Room.
Look but speak soft – ah, who would stir him
to suffer the more, his slumber so sweet.
He is sleeping, my Benoni.

He is sleeping, my Benoni! Now, with your unquiet hand,
lift up this curtain and look on his face –
his wide eyes shut, his brow part-paled.
How peaceful, and smiling perhaps… perhaps,
out of a pleasant dream. Listen! A sigh.

He is sleeping, my Benoni, Ah, sad disturber,
you call his name – leave him to absence.
You sob and you shudder , you kiss him

and pluck up the hand that pressed mine.
Do not rewake him... no need for a storm;
in your tempest of tears I too will be shaken.

He is sleeping, your Benoni:
I envy him such fair unfairness.
Poor boy – the mystery of life ungrasped,
his melancholy hour is early done:
the soul, thought-sundering the flesh,
takes to Heaven, ununderstood.
He is sleeping, our Benoni!

THE OLDEN CAPTAIN

'But at last the sailor cries
Land! Land! Look there!'
– Pierre-Jean de Béranger

John, my old salt, it must be France! France!
I smell it, like haler breath in our weary sails.
John, am I wrong?
Can you see, there in the fog that hides the harbour wall;
can you see, there aflutter – a dream! No dream!
He's back!

John, John, hug me, kiss me – ah,
mind my old wounds! – caper and trust me
and pipe happy tears.
Can you feel my heart hammer? I'm happy,
I'm happy that God gives His scullion
the sight of Him, fifteen years after all,
my old, exiled King!
He's back!

John, John, how stupid we were to think He was gone.
Somehow I knew in the end He'd come back
with his sword in his hand, from his empty inch,
starved of lordship and awe
to shake us awake with the voice that we knew.
He's back!

John, John, how stupid we were to think He was gone,
who plucked the hand of Rome to His crown,
and climbed to His throne on the ruin of kings,
unbloodied, unbotched,
unhavocked by cutthroats and dogs that eat dogs.
He's back!

John, John, how stupid we were to think He was gone,
who once with one shock-making wave
thunderbolted the world!
How ever could our Shepherd be dead?
Listen! The broken brig drowns in its storm;
and the rocks go down with a crack in their fall,
but He's back!

John, John, we are all for the passing,
but His will clatter the earth,
and there will be wonders, born of a howl,
wonders awful and new,
awful and new as the death of God,
that will rip up the world and the temple-blind.
He's back!

John, John, pull down the pennon, the colours we hate
and nail up this comet-flag
that sweet Heaven has sent us for revenge,
that stuns the eagle in sight of it, sudden to stop,
and the ocean to blow its top in hurrah!
He's back!

John, John, my heart is exploding with happiness –
look at it snapping there, its glory, its blue, its white and its
    red!
the flying redeemer!
that wraps in its long-house shroud
the palled old corpses, old kings, old Europe.
He's back!

John, John, run to the cannoners, tell them their homeland
has thrown off its yoke, and tell them to thunder
our freedom in shell and in shot!
and twenty times twenty let fly with their battery
to left and to right.
Ah God! this will be patience and patience discharged.
He's back!

John, John, who is that shouting down there on the strand?
a hundred times shouting the same, the same –
is it Him? No, no – 'tis a crowd-cry
angry and only for – freedom!
And… and… there on the top of their banner-jack
is that an eagle? I see the Lord's eagle
clutching at lightning, keeping the storm!

'No, no! It's the old French rooster, Commander' –
and the Captain he heard, and he blanched and back-footed,
and the two old salts, less hearty and fired now,
looked on each other in silent amaze,
crestfallen by nightfall, its reckless elation
like a girl hurling her arms
round the neck of her lover
to find she is kissing the enemy's lips.

A TIMELY CORRECTIVE

> *'Can't get her out of my heart;*
> *Or find a place for you'*
> – François de Malherbe

Don't call me cold, don't call me proud,
don't think my heart's a brazen door;
my eye aloof, my smile unkind,
my soul shut tight to soft desire.

You may know much, but not my mind:
think less that I am ice – I too
can love and burn, and promise to be true.

I love with gloomy majesty,
like kingdoms shot with bloody light:
alone, on some old balcony
my lute plucks forth its shimmered scales.

And hid from sight, I count the kisses
lovers share, while in the night
the floating moon rocks with silver light.

The hundred hunters bursting mud,
the brash horns winding in the woods,
the beaters and the howling hounds,
the hue, the cry, the bloody end.

And underneath the setting sun
the hillfolks pipe in glades unseen,
and tread their quiet measures on the green.

I love the fume of frankincense
and manna, and the sweet field-flowers;
to loll, half-nude, at hot midday
on plump divans in dizzy rest:

a pipe, a scented cigarette,
an aromatic tea, refined
to mollify my melancholy mind.

To plunder long-forgotten books
and find new liking in the dust;
unknot some Greek or Latin ode,
try a verse, unearth a gem:

and then the crazy, reeling feast,
the shameless orgy: as I read
my body sinks beneath the weight of greed.

And summer nights through woods and fields
agallop on my pelting bay;
songs of war that wake the steeps,
and fire, and flames! my darksome thrill.

To crush the tin god and his flag;
to splash the blade with blood; to break
the rash invader's heart, for freedom's sake.

Don't call me cold, don't call me proud,
don't think my heart's a brazen door;
my eye aloof, my smile unkind,
my soul shut tight to soft desire.

You may know much, but not my mind:
think less that I am ice – I too
can love and burn, and promise to be true.

THE WORKER'S HOLIDAY

to Joseph Bouchardi, Engraver

'Thus spake the lion'
– Phed.

'There is something rather ghastly about
Holy Love For Your Country'
– Louis de Saint-Just

Rest now, old poignard, good and faithful friend.
Rest, cradled in my hand; your country's light
and tired at last. Blood has rivered your blade,
which rings yet from a hundred shocks.

I am well content. We know each other's souls.
You ward my will; and when my killer's arm
thrusts you, throwing a glittered circle through the air,
you hurry forth, and in, to greedy death.

Rest now, old poignard, good and faithful friend.
Rest, cradled in my hand; your country's light
and tired at last. Blood has rivered your blade,
which rings yet from a hundred shocks.

And now you have had your fill. Your prey
has foundered at your feet. The streets are red.
And had your pleasure: to strike a tin god,
screeching twixt his bones, and nail death down.

Rest now, old poignard, good and faithful friend.
Rest, cradled in my hand; your country's light
and tired at last. Blood has rivered your blade,
which rings yet from a hundred shocks.

Such slaughter surely cannot be a crime.
Tread down my childhood, so, when I am a man
I break my chains and stir against the yoke. Beware!
Man counts his days of dirt, and waits his hour.

Rest now, old poignard, good and faithful friend.
Rest, cradled in my hand; your country's light
and tired at last. Blood has rivered your blade,
which rings yet from a hundred shocks.

So – see this cap that rides my shock?
'Tis triple-greased with spy-blood.
The scarlet grins at me: tis our banner,
the sainted surcoat of our chosen god.

Rest now, old poignard, good and faithful friend.
Rest, cradled in my hand; your country's light
and tired at last. Blood has rivered your blade,
which rings yet from a hundred shocks.

'Tis hung at my thigh; dear penetrator –
still you quiver, ready, and I clinch your steel.
And years to come I'll stud you with gems
like a hero's mettlesome blood-horse.

Rest now, old poignard, good and faithful friend.
Rest, cradled in my hand; your country's light
and tired at last. Blood has rivered your blade,
which rings yet from a hundred shocks.

THE MEETING-PLACE
To Eugène Bion, Monument-maker.

'by moonshine…'
– Argot

'Thus to the graveyard
one autumn dusk ghostly-grey,
a bier is borne!'
– Théophile Gautier

"You said: Fail me not, in the gloaming,
when the woodcutter hies to his home
and weary with toil at his table
shares his mite of broken bread,
bare profit of his bitter day,
among his little loving-ones,
who, careless of amibtion's sway, remain
darlinged in his modest care.

You said: I love you,
low and secret-sweet:
when the bells ring out in the tower,
seven strikes upon the murmuring air,
when beneath the gothic roodscreen's bow
the priest with humble hand
has swung the censer's smoking globe,
when beneath the guttered lamps
the widows reedy sing
'Te lucis ante terminum' –

You said: ah, come at such an hour,
silent by the wall of marbled knights,
past the gloomy hermit's cell

that lours beneath the poplars there;
then softly slip across the whispering ness
that beetles on the ever-beating lake,
its verdant forehead racked by southern gales,
towards this phantom willow, white
and jutty, crouched in gnomish wise,
charged with long and silver locks.

You said to me: but yet… what cruel arrest… ?
Ah, fatal visions crowd my mind!
Infernal Gods! How must we wait!
How we must bear this fevered rage!
To cloak the long, untimely dark
and hush the restless torchlight of my soul,
that longs to brighten so at beauty's sight,
I weave the great-leafed lilies here,
that often you have laden in your arms,
a green bed for our love beneath this shade.

You said:… how time decays!
I wait… you have not come.
The moonlight gasps upon my armoured breast,
sure bright enough to beckon you.
A rival! Ah – betrayed!"

He staggers back, returns, retreats,
his spurs jangle harshly
and, furious at tether-end,
he thrusts his lance into the earth
and with his dagger tears the darkling trees.

And suddenly he sees a light,
which flits beyond, towards the manse:
a coffin glides towards the churchyard,

a coffin pale and – "ah! who comes behind?
God! God! – it is your father there,
who weeps at Heaven and toils to walk –

I doubted you! – so – Doubter! on your knees
and, dagger – strike! Thus!
and tear my throat, and chase your steel in blood.

Together! At our Meeting-Place!"

A PICTURE OF ISEULT
to Jehan Duseigneur, sculptor

'And chaste love grows the heart'
– Victor Hugo

Dear gift of love's bright flame, in whose
bronze and emerald round there shines the fair
Iseult, angel of melancholy mien:
ah, let me press my lips upon that face,
allow me yet that sweet indulgence,
purest pleasure – which is all I seek!
For who would dare his fingers there
to touch, and fright so fair a child?

I look at her, and I am overcome,
like some grey palmer praying to a chapel spire:
so heavenly my soul and breath are lost,
so pure my heart is purified,
so holy that I drink from its bright chalice.
And thus let me adore this languished flower
that hearkens at its golden morning-tide.
No flower's crown shone so in such a round!

How can the soul be safe?
Ah, leave your mumbling sermons for the grave,
take reverence from this face that you revere;
eternity is long enough, and it will serve.
Stay here, and end your exile from our sight,
bright shadow! Angel angels tend!
Walk still among us. You have your servant now.
He understands: so softly tell the story of your dream,

that he may lead your too distracted way
and end your sad, distempered solitude.
Heaven's picture! Picture well-beloved!
Maid with honey-breath of absent words!
This picture is a lovesong for my heart
whose notes are cradled, scented, in the air.

Who made me this? This little, tender treasure
and all its fair delights? – Jehan!
My dear friend, Jehan, whose nimble chisel
has woken Abelard from blocks of stone,
Hugo, Calvin, Esmeralda, Roland,
mighty as Homer, and as Virgil grand.

DESPAIR

to Giulio Piccini, Maestro

> 'Ever a gust of flames beneath the heaving breath
> Seeks to prison my agitated soul...'
> – Théophile Dondey, 'Insomnie'

Like a she-wolf tired with empty hunt,
that grates her teeth and turns upon her way,
I turn too, charged with trouble, wasted pale
and all alone: no hand in mine,
no voice that whispers – *ah, tomorrow!*

Yet some life-sap surges in me still.
Oh, women! My poor heart can also love!
Twenty, favoured-fair – I should be loved,
should have pleased, at least, so courteous-kind –
but none have come, to cross my lonely Fate.

And this too-taxing torment grates and tears my soul
and crushes me entire! Ah, my wounding Fate!
which just today, my baffled hunt cast off
and ready more to bathe my heart in gall,
set me an angel fair before my eyes.

Ah, ravishment! The dreaming guise, the dreaming song,
and at her dreaming steps I sensed a certain joy.
Hot-mouthed, I took her gown against my lips
and reeling with the flowers' tidal scent
I felt my heart engorge. And yet, and yet...

how soon this moment withered; how awful
my spent waking – and I looked for her in vain,
my eye greedy with foolish fire, but she was gone.
Ah make her back, you rhadamanthine gods!
Cast this pretty prey before my hungered heart!

My sad, frustrated fury somersaults my soul
that wished for flesh submissive to its chase,
and maddened by desire I – ah, infamous!
To rip a woman from her dotard's arms,
to rip… but no, no, to heel, you hounds!

Insistent, sad desires, be still. Keep to your hide.
And I shall burn with flame unsatisfied
and tiptoe wounded to my single bed
and weep away my too exhausted flesh.
My heart has broken in this hunt.

My meagre years insist, and wear me down:
ah, give me the sage acceptance of old men.
What am I doing here? To drag myself from pain to pain?
Too fearful soul!… Let us be free, and break our chains!
Now!… My pistols!… here… at last… and thwart mischance!

WHIMSY

Birds! Birds! I wish I was one!
The merriest creatures under the sun!

Your sky-easy tacking, your casual care,
Your feathers that fly without Wisdom or God,
Dizzy as cloudlets and fair-weather-shod!
Your trilly fly-hunting that jingles the air!

Birds! Birds! I wish I was one!
The merriest creatures under the sun!

Your games in and out of the gates of the sky!
Your unvarnished voices the Soul understands,
Like echoes of Promised and faraway lands
Where our thoughts and our words are a bitterless sigh!

Birds! Birds! I wish I was one!
The merriest creatures under the sun!

Free of need and jealousies;
Free of ambition and free of pain;
Free of prisons and free of chains;
Free of Bishops and Majesties!

Birds! Birds! I wish I was one!
The merriest creatures under the sun!

No Princes, no Heroes, no Conquering Lords,
No brain-withered Judges with cobwebs for hearts;
No bickering families to tear you apart;
No plotting relations, no ropes and no swords!

Birds! Birds! I wish I was one!
The merriest creatures under the sun!

No flesh-creeping lusts, no voluptuous wrongs;
No slave-making marriage, no Oaths to deny;
Happy in Liberty! Wild as the sky!
Long live your freedom! and long live your songs!

Birds! Birds! I wish I was one!
The merriest creatures under the sun!

CORSICA

to Napoléon Thom, painter

> *'He's just a painter, Lord, who calls himself Romano, and lives by the*
> *quiet plunder of Nature, and has no weapons but his brushes'*
> – Friedrich Schiller, *Fiesque*, Act II

The mistral blew: the lilac welkin
glittered like sunstone with a thousand stars.
The boatman's song faded at the shore
and sombre silence hung upon the land.
Among the distant mountain-folds
only the bandits' whistle… wheep… and wheep.

The ocean heaved, the sobbing waves rushed back…
and ramped again on the shore, like the furious stramash
loosed by galléd kings upon the land
against the Lion-heart of this unkneeling isle.
Who, being there, could not have thought
the whole world roused to the sky!

The thick horizon pressed itself against the mighty
wall of hills, and mountains, rocks and shattered shards
that lays along the Corsic ridge like giant limbs
and watches from Bonifacio the Sardinian strand
to Bastia, that lifts, from gentler seawash,
its silver forehead to the sky.

The people slept, and all was still. But near
the meagre doorway of his humble cot
old Viterbi sat, the tireless hunter,
whose arm ne'er hurt another's, a broad old hat
upon his head, soft-shining now
luminous with locks of silver-white.

And in this solitary place, before his sleep,
bent upon his musket, eyes fixed on the ground,
he breathed the evening's sweet and living air –
and then, far off, a *flash* of sworded flame,
as if a child's soul were plucked by God above.
He crossed himself with lowered head.

And suddenly, he heard… and stood… and listened yet…
the grate of footsteps on the stony track.
'Who's there! Show yourself! And are ye French?
A friend? Oh foolish friend to walk these darkling combes
unarmed! Stranger, beware the sudden knife,
the cut-throat and the open way to death!'

I am, he said, *a painter, at my own business,*
returning from the valley where I sat to draw.
Good sir, I am a Frenchman through and through.
I walk here free of fear, though it be night,
beneath my cloak, see, only my palette:
my baggage is no threat or arms.

'But know you must that Corsica desires revenge,
not money. Ah, may the wrong-doer beware!
If you be Death's sweet prey, it will figure your steps
through the woods, through the world, like a greedy hyena;
He will wait month on month till his victim comes by
to be skewered on his own foul deeds.

Walking here, alone and unarmed on this darkling path,
you should sing, my friend, or perhaps, in these shadows,
the bandits may take you for somebody else: march!
and sing! or whistle those songs that my weathered old soul
loved well at your age – the songs of your country,
the dirges of tyrants and kings!

Ah, callow! We feared no man, and caution despised!
But an old man's words are thought to be dotage:
and the heart that boils with life has no care.'
And the young painter, when the old man was done,
taking no notice, walked on, saying no word,
and smiling at nothing, and passed into dark.

But near to Oletta, a sharp surge of fear
clutched at his heart. A noise. Some noise. *Ah,*
only the olive-trees. But maybe – maybe – a knife-thrust
under the branches! I shake like a child!
And the passing thought passed, and the reaching fingers,
the low-tongued voice, are only the whisper of waves.

But hardly had he fallen back into happier thought
than a musket-shot knocked him sudden athwart
and down! – and his cry tore the air, and at it a laugh,
cruel and short, and a shadow flung near and cut out his throat.
'The Devil! What have I done! Mistook my man!
This is not the old fellow, Viterbi the dotard!'

And he snapped his sword in his heartsick rage,
and slipped swiftly away under the jag-toothed rocks…
And the passer-by in the morning next saw only
a cloak stiff with blood, a sketchbook's tatters,
the ghastly remnants of half-gnawed bones
and a shattered skull scattered across the path.

THOUGHTS AND PAIN

'I am crushed with sadness'
– Rudiment

I hear the virginals. Unwelcome happy notes,
what do you want of me?
Have you climbed to my attic to over-madden my mind?
My too, too-battered heart?

Such happy sounds. Begone. And pour this surging joy on
    other men,
whose lives are festal feasts
where I have not intruded; intrude now not on my distress,
my private miseries!

Oh, indiscrete! Who conjures you? What white hand?
What fingers prisoned with gems
tap upon your board
of ivory and ebon thus?

Are you the ground for some sweet angel-child
in his hesitant lesson?
Ah, only if the air is sad, the beating hand dismayed,
beguile me with his song.

No, no. I hear the muffled tread of whirling crowds
in a tiny drawing-room;
they float and spin in straitened riot,
shaking the roof and walls.

Without, a swing of sounds and cries, horse-shrieks,
plaits of flowers, footmen, fiery brands:
the Rich disgorge their pleasures, and the poor
weep ashamed beneath their rags.

And all about me, palaces! Sickly courtesy,
possessions, nights of over-much.
Hope, splendour, honour: amidst such a world
I am only pale and poor.

They are there, ah, the great, the kings, the canting priests,
in Execution Square,
whose pomp is come to taste wrung blood –
a Jew on the fire!

The world kills me: nothing, misery, want,
my days decay in gobbets!
My golden loves are sewn upon my life's black fustian.
No more! Ah, no more love.

Poor thing. I dragged you heedless still
along the path of pain.
And you, before my poison killed you,
ended all with other.

And still with this sharp steel
I hesitate – a child, a capon and a churl! –
to rip this coward's heart
from out its plaguey breast!

But mull upon my miseries, their shadows hand in hand
with inescapable lament.
So weak I am, and why? What irons keep me here?
A sorry, muck-heap Job.

VICTORY
to P…

> *'Ma'am, your kindness,*
> *Give me your kindness…'*
> – Alphonse Broy

> *Stay me with flagons, comfort me with apples: for I am sick of love.*
> – Bible

Now leave me, for the night is late.
Our moon has suddenly bedimmed.
Now leave me, though the road is dark
and I afraid. What use are we?

No more those blithe, unwanted kisses,
staining friendship's lips with love.
Too much fire! You break your vow,
and kindness teeters to desire.

Now leave you? It grows late? Ah, cruel,
I burn to love you rather! Long
I waited: please, no more 'tomorrow'.
Grant me your lips, your neck, your hand:

And when my heart is full, my hands
shall stroke your silken gown and – no!
Unsatisfied! I need you all!
All! Good sir, you paw in vain!

No bleats! No tears! Ah, brute! *Ah, lady –*
only cries of ecstasy!

THE SOLITARY

'The mighty woods reborn,
The quiet valleys round:
All compassed are with fear'
– Pierre de Ronsard

Beneath the sun-struck gales of tropic climes,
where Afric backs are bowed to English canes,
in beating light the palms luxuriant
swarm their woody limbs toward the vines.

Here, the succubitic mistletoe
in ancient woods entwines the noble oak,
its nodding creepers bound for life unto
the sacred bole that shares their single fate.

Vine, palm and mistletoe, would I were thee!
My lonely heart desires thy keen embrace,
to softly staddle me the stream of life:
a woman or a friend to bear me on!

Perhaps some earthly angel… flower-maid…
Ah, poet! In this maddened whirl of world
that dances to the clattered virginals,
come choose! No, no. 'Tis my *soul* miscarries.

Not at some babbled revels, or the stage,
will I discover one who shores my heart:
but in the darkling meadows, sweetly shawled,
with *Werther*, 'neath the weeping-willow's shade.

No ravened lass with fluttered, jetty eyes,
but some luxuriant swan, a blue-eyed sprite,
whose look is almond-soft and full of care,
that muses sad reflections in the stream.

When will she come? She has not answered yet,
nor brought her Springtime soul unto my heart
that 'til the cypress-shades of Death would love.
But on the shore I wait alone and pine.

The sparrows sleep together on my roof;
my mare has lent her body to the steed;
yet I, in my still-solitary bark,
waste all my days upon the urgent stream.

THE BARON'S DAUGHTER
to Théophile Gautier, poet

Ah, give me back my bonny Guy:
my humble heart is his for aye!

Dry your tears, beloved daughter,
take my treasure, what you will;
will you pass the sun? – Behold!
Coin and velvet, rings and gold!

Ah, give me back my bonny Guy:
my humble heart is his for aye!

Daughter, can you love this gowk,
and set at naught Lord Archambult?
whose mighty weapon stands so near
the throne, and who the King holds dear?

Ah, give me back my bonny Guy:
my humble heart is his for aye!

He has three castles in Touraine,
and towering two beside the Rhone,
and you a Lady there would be,
and shine in gentil company.

Ah, give me back my bonny Guy:
my humble heart is his for aye!

And all would grovel at your feet
as if you were a hallowed Queen,
and kiss your traces in the sand
when you go riding on the strand!

Ah, give me back my bonny Guy:
my humble heart is his for aye!

Ach! Deny us to your death,
ye Honourless! My vassals now
drag her to her dungeon cell
and toll the iron passing-bell!

Ah, give me back my bonny Guy:
my humble heart is his for aye!

THE RAMPARTS
to Augustus Mac-Keat, poet.

*'For lo, the winter is past, the rain is over and gone… arise, my love,
and come away…'*
– Bible.

'… and soft embraces…'
– Giovanni Boccaccio

Give me your hand, my dear, and sit us down
beside this clattered paling. See the village there,
hanging midst the cloughs like some giant-child's toy block;
dream of ancient Babel's ramping tower;
a captive of the mountains' rocky steeps;
an archway worn with all the great world's waves .

Listen! Far-off echoes of hurrahs and clatterings;
the clamorous calls from cliff to castle wall;
the restless helms, the musket-thickets' hum;
the dinned portcullis and the grinding gates.
It seems the keep is strewn with glittered gems,
whose fires outnumber festivals of kings.

So, I am to heel: my forced indifference
contents you. But for me – I rage, I burn;
to be alone in company with you, and stay my blood!
Ah no, it cannot be. This brother-love
breaks upon your beauty, and my promises are naught.
They were not made for you. I die in flames!

O childlike, how should you obey the bestial
and cock-eyed laws, and bow to such inconsequence
the world that spurns us still contrives as virtues
that would make your God to blush! Do you believe
that Nature's voice is trumpery? Oh end this cruelty, my dear,
or else your kingdom will be nought but broken walls.

This love that you decline unwelcomely
inhabits you, your nature all proclaims its kind;
your breasts' sweet swell, your half-smiled lips,
your light-tipped tread, your ripe-veiled indolence,
your musicked voice, your vague, caressing hand…
all, all compel to service even he, the most unbowed.

Before us, lovers, passing happy through the whispered grass,
have – sure, you know the words, my dear – *made merry*.
What might betray you then? This place is sure no pandar.
Now you weep: and I am drunk with joy!
Your quiet sobs sugar my bittered heart,
and in the burning circle of your arms I choke with ecstasy!

O Night, who was so long the echo of my torment,
now draw on, draw out, and thicken this delight!
How long our waiting; how short our fading then.
And I would bless and I would clutch the cannonball
that came to blast our tomb, and lay us in.
Ah, to die, to die, sans sword, sans help, sans all!

DAYDREAMS

'All dies'
– Gerard

'The world's a cheat'
– from *The Imitation of Jesus Christ,* verse translation by Pierre
Corneille

Death is the Moral that hangs on the Fable of life;
and Life a sudden strait accounted out
in mile-stones, where soon and oft the armèd hero falls
in sudden splendour – ah, enviable fate!
The world is an Ocean where life's humble brig
creeps ragged from the quay beyond the heads;
where the bold buccaneer sails beneath the equatorial sun,
glutted with suppliant blood and golden ransom.
Death! Great executioner!… Ah, no, no – an empty nothing,
a ditch where all go down… the coward's cry unheeded in
      the dark!
And all the same beneath its punctual axe,
both man and dog!

All, aye, all. The great, the weak, the passer-by:
from general destruction springs new life
which soon itself is utterly destroyed.
Come to the earth and, suffering, die: for this man knows
is how things be. Existence is a volume
man cannot decipher, its chapters writ in Arab wise
and given to a muleteer. The title and the end alone
he understands: the rest is vacancy, by way of every word.
Some say the Earth's brief man is its ambitious Pilgrim:
ah, perhaps – but where is Compostella, where is Mecca,

what Heaven's inn lies open to his deathless soul?
None. 'Tis nothing all.

About me, see! the strutting multitudes
press near, and all their hopeful hearts are voids.
Tell me where the rotted trunk of this old oaktree goes –
it goes in smuts to fatten up the earth: and you, brave stump,
a monster by the name of God has held for you a later fate!
Ah, race of trodden men, be not so proud,
for soon your grinning, white, chap-fallen skull
will be a toy for children of your town,
and not one jot will matter then to you – your useless bone
draggled in the mud by one, and slapped and chipped by more…
No matter, ha! come Judgement Day – taraaa! –
it is reborn.

THE ADVENTURER

'Can I not go and smoke the cigar of my existence where I will?'
– A Famous Writer

This suffocating sand cannot be crossed.
Two nights have passed since first I left its shore;
westwards I walk, and am not out of it.
My feet sink hopeless deeper in its waste,
my staff is broken and my body fails;

and now, quite worn, I sit and wait to die,
alone as some old ruin's ghostly shade
amidst this nothing, shelterless and wide.
With blanken stare I contemplate the earth
that stretches endless as a giant sheet…

Nothing but my thirst and me; and silence –
only my breath and beating heart. Ah, God!
I topple, weak and bent with pain. How small
is man in such immensity. Ah, God!
How feeble in the face of sorrow's breath.

Blaspheme and weep, presumptuous Traveller,
wake now from your desperate dream of gold…
My end deserved, and yet deserved the more:
my father pining unto death, and I,
unfeeling, clutch at wealth, and find it Death.

SONG TO THE SUN
to André Borel

Here on this empty path, the lonely track
of my unfigured woes,
I, weeping, come, and lay down on the earth
like any animal.

I come to cheat my hunger, and to sleep
all pillowed round with stones:
to shut my withered eyelids sure;
to claim my scot of sun!

Down there, the avaricious kings demand
their chary-sparing tithes,
and sell the sun and nothings to their sheep.
But I have paid my part.

And on us all, all equal now, the sun
depends its generous light,
which is not dearer to a Lord's display
than to its ragged friend.

HAPPINESS AND NO
to Philadelphe O'Neddy, poet

> *'One makes himself a Lordling fit for minstrelsy,*
> *The next a Duke, the next a Family Tree'*
> – Mercier

I have caressed my death, and smiled at self-slaughter
so many times when I was more content,
when, staled in dull enjoyment, indifferent and dull,
I wearied of the long blue sky, and of a lover's bed.

Ah, happiness is heavy, it sends our souls to sleep;
it fetters hearts with iron bands
it muffles up the oars that speed the ship of life
and tramples underfoot the flames of Hell,

the flaming halo of the poet's thought –
its sacred brand cast from the temple's front.
False friend! For from the Persian casket of his mind
there winds a perfume passioning to Man.

He is a bird! and must stay wild and free.
At night, beneath the woodland brake, he sings:
a muddied snipe that struts the river's bank
and greets the sunrise and the setting light.

He is a bird! and must grow old with care,
quiet, poor, unknown, shy and sad,
and singing all alone, with nothing in this world
but just a ragged cloak, a dudgeon, and the sky!

And yet the Poet Now sings namby-pamby,
corseted in tame-to-please, a spruced and mealy smile,
a parrot warbling for Society,
a private canary in a golden cage:

a fat and greasy hoofer turning on the tears
for common-safe complaints that follow ten-course meals,
waving an umbrella, and swearing on his sword,
his potions in his hand, requiring death –

and diamonds, balls and flowers, horses, keeps and damsels
people all his thundersinking verse.
And naught to Poverty, nought to common plight,
but ever with his velvet glove of words another blow.

Ah, suffocate your autocratic airs!
Ye snatchers of sad flotsam from the wreckage!
Cast off your tricks and trifles, buttons, braids,
these lines that make the ragged man to blush.

Ah, ye counterfeited suns, baa-lambs and fakes!
Hide not your own ashamèd beggary:
for not from this pretence will ye find truth.
The poet is refined by need's intoxicate.

I have caressed my death, and smiled at self-slaughter
so many times when I was more content...
and now I hate the thought, and am afraid,
too poor, and sapped by hunger's casualty.

A LITTLE ODE

Ah! I wish I was a troubadour,
a gentil Medieval bard!
And whilst the bondsmen moil at work and war,
my labour and my love should be, forsooth,
my lute, my lady, and a Poet's Truth!

Beneath my mantle thus I bear my dower:
my lute to pluck for bed and sack,
my glaive to grasp before my lady's bower!
The sheathèd warrant of her life and fee;
unsheathèd in the cause of Liberty!

AT THE WINDOW
to Alphonse Brot, poet

'Long I listened, and came to think the harmony was me...'
– Georges Buffon

I love to dream a day away in gentleness alone,
sitting at my window in the evening breeze,
free of care complete, in some sweet reverie,
my softly-opened soul an elsewhered ecstasy,
beneath whose quiet hand my being glides as one
and murmurs like a lyre in kindly harmonies.

There, leant amongst the flowers of a spreading apricot
whose tangled branches whisper on the walls,
I feel the world dissolve and die, while I,
king for a day, attend the funeral of the earth,
which distantly the monastery bell proclaims,
and dreamy watch the little dog, the crow,
the mule, that linger lately on the lawns.

But more than this, no painter could describe my joy
when through the branches some white-slender form
appears before my dazzled eyes and seems to flutter
branch to branch, her voice, in sweetest harmony,
like to the plaintive reed, plays trippingly
and rises like a perfume to my hearkening brow.

Ecstatic and intoxicate, no worldliness remains,
and through my weightless flesh my flooded soul
turns, drop by drop, to dew: and like the bright strings
of a silver lute that throbs beneath the hand
of some grace-leaning angel, all the earth trembles and dissolves.
I am a sound: a shadow-sight: a mystery...

Perhaps you, worldly, smile at this fond power,
so strong, so otherworldly, on my soul –
the simple whisper of a woman's gown
as lately she steps through the half-lit night –
that this should move me so – a jewelled hand, a throat
where pearls and gems whisper like a stream –
that these should move me so!

Ah! the innocent, the plain, unknowing heart
may feel these draughts of love, these drunken reels.
And who, uncoarsened now with wine and lust
could not see in this setting sun the fairest joy?
Let him come tomorrow: I will wait, here, at my window,
and soon his youngling soul will burn like mine.

ON THE JURY'S REJECTION OF THE PAINTING 'THE BAILIFF'S DEATH'

'Tears are sweeter than 'tis thought'
– Francesco Petrarca

Dear Boulanger, my friend, you are disappointed.
I am with you in your black windway.
Let me add my anger to your baffled plaint;
let me thrash your vile executioners;
let me hammer infamy into their skulls
and rack them, and drag them to the meeted ways
and the People's Bench, where lies are shunned,
and there fling their hoggish sentence back in their face.

For now is the time we must shrivel with sunlight
these lackeys that lick at the arsehole of Power;
these decadent ants with their simperous hamming
that grovel to Bankers, and dance for a coin!
Bilge of the Empire, assassins of hope,
who have ground their own hearts into dust.
Bilge of the Past, sacked by our century,
fake Romans, fake Greeks, fake art and fake lives!

Kings self-appointed, their crowns in their hands,
hollow and dead as their rancorous polls,
who sit in a gaggle and squirm on their thrones
as the new generation advances its tide.
Like sick-stricken bears seeking blood in the woods
they follow, death-breathed, their prey to devour,
and crush in their arms, and tear in their School-yard,
all that is upright before they expire.

Ah, these are your Judges! The moth-eaten Court
that were taken with fear at the sight of your Art,
and pernicket its desolate, terrible tale:
O the People are ugly! The Bailiff so fair!
Their posturing lies, and their Policy hid.
Since when, my dear Critics, has your love of the People
so exercised you? Are you Jacobite now, ye dogs of the soul,
to slobber the Populace? Wicked! O, sly!

Thus weaselling, thus the Anathema said
on your labour, my friend, they hounded it out,
your page of good hope; the silent intent
of your brush so exact that they need call it lies.
Ha! Thus do the Mongers thrust Christ from the Temple!
Grrr! The day of our vengeance is near:
their tombs are half-yawning, their doors creaking wide,
and their works and their lives will go down in the dark.

To my dear friend, Jules Vabre:
excellent marrow!
with your little spyglass
on the Fat-Well-Off and their big-bald chins –
you and I must be Martians
on this pale and ordered Earth!
Ah, we must be emmets,
doing what we will, here,
in this pithless Paris,
hither and thither like haywisps on water,
like tonic eddies
through a fly-blown swamp.
Ramblers sans rooves, pewless and
popped from our containers
to live! live slaphappily
like sparrers dancing
on chimneytops!
Wildcats waiting in the wings,
the goggling crowd,
and then, up-curtains please!
we cross
the light-lit stage of Life.

AGATHA: A FRAGMENT
To Jean Borel

AGATHA *(alone, seated at a table)*:
No, no, it is not settled thus; no, no, it cannot be!
My tears and kisses fall in vain; ah, how should I agree:
my fate lies in your hands, I know, my life in your decree.
My life! My life! that you would stain – that you would pluck
    from me!
You wish to sack my breaking heart, you wish to break my
    will,
but I am free, yet free! I am… I am a woman still!
Should I be taken prisoner? Surrender to this vow?
I scorn it all, and vow against my too-rash promise now.
Ah, all I swore at mother's knee, and all I swore to her
I shall forget. I have forgot. The task is bitter, Sir:
that I, so young, so gentle, should to dotage thus be tied,
entombed alive! Ah, dreadful thought. The earth's untimely
    bride!
For I would wither in the clime of such a wintry bed,
beneath the senile kisses, ah, the kisses of the dead!

(She rises in agitation)

What have I said? Hush now ye words that kill my parent's
    heart!
Ah, father dear, forgive me now, for too soon we must part.
Ah yes, my fate is welcome now! Who would not envy me?
For thus can I acquit the debt that sets my parent free.

If I should spurn this cruel man, alas, if I should falter,
you die upon the scaffold! Ah! now drag me to the altar,
bring flowers, bring my wedding-gown, for I shall be a wife
and I shall speak the fatal word that tolls the end of life!
Such they wish. Such I will do. And thus without regret.

(with bitterness)

His ghastly hair is white as bones; it breathes the scent of
    death,
and little time shall I endure alive his coffin'd breath.
Ah! what merry marriages do families arrange!

(she sits at the virginals)

'Tis nine o'clock. Ah, Adrian, you are not come. 'Tis strange;
you promised, dear, upon the hour. Ah, love, what keeps you
    now?
And yet, dear friend, be slower yet, another hour allow
with dragging step; and at the feet of she who loves you well
learn soon enough whom Fate removes, and list the passing
    knell
for those who die as It demands. Ah, soon enough, my
    friend.
Come not to my embrace, ah, love, come not to condescend
your ills. I am no longer thine. Go seek another's chains!
Ah God! I tremble now. Alas! This fatal thought remains:
whilst dreams of Spring and sunlit life come back and cradle
    me
with their deceits that conjure in my heavy heart – but see!

a brief, sweet smile, a second's light, a transient caress…
my blood is up, I wait and burn, and burn the more from
    this –
that Adrian will come and soothe my madness with a kiss.
Come, let us pluck the crownèd flower of love's sweet holiday.
Ah, Adrian, 'tis dark now, and I cannot find the way.
Come let us quench the fiery pain that doubles in my breast.
See how my fingers tremble on these keys, and cannot rest.
How hum and drum my voiceless words, how heavily they
    weigh.
What matter! Come sweet music, help me smile. Ah, let me
    play.
A painèd heart may rest amongst another harmony!

(the doors is shaken from without)

I hear the door. Who is it? Ah, who is it? It is he!

(she opens the door softly)

Who is it? Speak… who is it?…

ADRIAN *(merrily)*:
                              Ah, 'tis Adrian! 'Tis I!
AGATHA:
You come in shadows silent here, beneath a silent sky.

ADRIAN *(entering):*
Beneath the tower I stood awhile, like to a troubadour,
and listened to my lover's song and to her steps before.
Ah, if you knew how much, upon the Devil of my heart,
the voice of Woman whispers her intoxicating Art!
That song I never heard before. You sang it not for me.
Ah, teach it me… ah, teach me now! –

(he embraces her gently)

AGATHA:

                        Impatient! Let me be!

ADRIAN:
Ah no, this dish is mine: its sauce quite to my taste. And I
will sup of it, delirious, and feast upon a sigh.

(he sits upon her lap)

AGATHA:
Ah, forward! Come then, sit upon my lap, my sweet, you may
   –
the pantry is not locked, my dear. Ah, what will people say!

ADRIAN:
Their words would jealous be, and we the sowers of that seed,
and keep our harvest close in fantasies of golden greed!
But what a solemn face you have, your eyes are filled with
    tears.
What troubles you, my darling, ah, what tongueless frights
    and fears

disturb you now? You answer not. My hand beats in your
    hand.
No answer yet. We are alone. I do not understand:
I kneel before you now – 'Tis me! Some dire offence of mine!
Will you not tell me, trust me, dear? You know my soul is
    thine.

AGATHA:
Dear friend… my love, henceforth I fear I cannot well be
    yours,
for I must be another's prize, and for another's cause.

ADRIAN *(interrupting)*:
The Devil! Who? Who then?

(he lays hands upon his sword)

                            Ah, here, my hand takes up
    my sword,
whose steely blade shall end of fever of this sickly bawd!
Name him! Now name this knave, this monstrous varlet.
    Name him now!
That –

AGATHA *(seriously)*:
              Hush, it is a dotard lord I may not disallow.
Oh Adrian, now hear, my dear and blameless father's fate,
who, brave and loyal, to escape the headsman's axe – which
    late
the subtle Cardinal hung o'er him – keeping by good chance

a knife to serve him for a cross, the dangered cause of France –
this vicious France, that mocks the king, and calls him renegade,
that licks like mongrel bitches at the axeman's bloody blade –
fled, I say, from Richelieu. To save his hunted head
he hurried safe to old Turin; and in this kindless stead,
which he thought filled with likesome friends, and safe for
    sanctuary,
obscure and quiet, hid from harm, he thought, to safely tarry
and end the last short days that God allowed – ah, misled!
For Richelieu, espying how the prey whose counted head
he thirsted for, with mighty bruit set on the chase again,
to find the butcher's meat, my parent dear, and have him slain.
Orlando, Lord of old Turin, the ancient, grim and grey,
did lust for me – and shamed his honour – ah, alas the day!
And, dear, I know not why, took my refusal for a slight,
and moiled my father thus: *Agatha shall be mine tonight!*
Richelieu demands your head, and I demand a wife.
Which shall it be? Choose now, I say: your daughter or your life.
I fell at old Orlando's feet with fainting heart, and said:
To save my father's forfeit life, I will Orlando wed –
a villain faithless, Cardinal, as thee, and no less black.
And is my father's life to you at auction cheap, alack!
Well then, I shall be yours. Now take your wife and set him free,
upon your word and mine, your oath to me and mine to thee.
So he is saved, within my walls will your dear father stay.
And Richelieu cried out in vain for blood, and went his way.

So see his ring, and I am his, and soon we shall be wed,
as Spring to Winter. All my hateful tale thus have I said
without all want, with open heart, and told you what is true:
and this I do for love of him, and more for love of you.
And I am broken-hearted too, for, dear, I truly know
that in the beauty of your love you blame me not. And, oh,
how beautiful it is to know that you would this advise

had you been there, my dear. Come to me now, in friendly wise,
and take my – ah! what jealous, silent eyes – my sacrifice
is less than yours? What lesser torture comes at lesser price?
What terror could be more? What world so dark? What fear
    so great?
Ah, think upon the black, eternal torments that await!
Adrian, you shall be free, and free of stain and oath,
free for other promises, and free for pleasure both.
You can forget me now –

(Adrian stamps in anger and paces up and down the chamber)

                                    ah, pardon. What offence is mine?
Time dulls the world and all that passes there, and all resign
their loves… Come then and talk to me. Pace not so up and
    down,
it frightens me… that agitated step… that darkling frown…
Come sit with me, dear Adrian, and let me tell you true,
while we together are, how much I love and honour you.
Ah, time has wings and we a moment. Think on what we swore,

and let us say Farewell: a sweet embrace – then nothing more!
Now let us seal our honour and our faith with one last kiss –
until – ha! Yes! Death has claimed the dotard's soul, and this,
my shamed imprisonment, is done and he extinguished quite,
then shall I be yours for aye, and you reclaim your right,
if you still have me in your heart. If you remember me.

ADRIAN *(in fury)*:
Traitor!

AGATHA:

        Ah, who comes? Who thunders at the door? Ah,
it is he!

ADRIAN:
What blackguard at this hour?

AGATHA:

        O rash intruder! Fly, oh fly!
'Tis old Orlando – hide, hide here! Our Devil now draws nigh!

ADRIAN:
Ha! Your doddering wretch, your laughingstock! I shall not
hide.

ORLANDO *(without)*:
Open ho!

AGATHA:

        Orlando! Ah, the window lies awide –
O fly, my Adrian!

ADRIAN:

        You Gods! Upon his hour! 'Tis he!
(drawing his sword)
So let your hoary bridegroom come – to his eternity!
(Adrian puts his hand upon the bolt. Agatha takes him by the arm)

AGATHA *(softly)*:
Stop, Adrian, put by your sword. Cannot you understand?
By this you kill my father and my soul in one rash hand!

ORLANDO *(at the door)*:
Agatha! Open ho!

ADRIAN:

Now let him die.

AGATHA:

O, pity me!
O stop, my love, here let me kneel and pray. I love you. See!
(She swiftly takes the sword from his hand)

I have it!

(Agatha breaks the sword against the wall)
Ha! now strike him down if this will serve you
right!

ORLANDO:
Open in the name of God…

AGATHA *(pulling Adrian to the balcony)*:
Go vengeful! Leave my sight,
or I am lost!

(Agatha tidies her clothes and opens the door)

Good Sir, I am your servant. What you will.

ORLANDO *(enters, breaking the jewel-box he was carrying)*:
And are you deaf?

AGATHE *(innocently)*:
I minded here my prayers unfinished still.

ORLANDO:
I heard them… Ha! I heard…

AGATHA:
                           What did you hear, my
   Lord?

ORLANDO:
                                      My name.

AGATHA *(sweetly):*
Oh, jealousy! I prayed for you, dear Sir. Is God to blame?

THREE VILLANELLES

Don Aléjo smiles menacingly from out his cape
– Augustus Mac-Keat

The Old Breton Fiddler

to Henri de Labattut

Come, Bretons! 'Neath the maple-tree
come dancing to the bagpipes' skirl,
come sing and smile, come trip and twirl,
as in my Spring I danced like thee.

But now, alas, the grave is nigh,
my fingers cratch, my fingers craw;
come, follow, 'fore my time is o'er,
and take my dear old tunes for aye!

Do not forget thy dauntless name,
the meadows sweet that gave ye birth,
these blessed fields, this happy earth
that bore a thousand sons of fame!

Ah, Freedom guards thy Summer-land,
its mighty boughs about thy shore,
where Breton's Eagle rides once more –
and holds your promise in his hand!

Upon the mountains' flinty height
still lie the cairns and barrows old
where ancient Druid bards foretold
thy forebears' fates, thy fathers' plight!

Ye Saxons, grim of mien and eye
that some new Caesar still would know,
thy tongue unchanged – thy warlords so
called forth their warriors to die!

But day is done. The shadows creep,
our houses dull with misty shades;
now let us leave these spirit-glades
to darkling witchmen whilst we sleep.

Upon the tops the shadows run,
the dwarves are dancing 'bout the stones!
The eagles scream, the forest moans –
home! ye Bretons! Day is done.

The Birth of a Countess

'Most excellent!' – my friends
'A trifle!' – my friends

Oh, Manon dear, what have you done?
Your neckerchief is all a-bunch.
Your jerkin has a horrid stain
all down the back. I think it's grass.
Picking filberts by the weir?
At midnight? Oh, come come, my dear.
You little saucebox. Ah, I fear
you have a taste for it. Heigh-ho!

Ho-hum, you seem a little damp,
your face a little pale and green
about the gills – at seventeen!
Oh, Manon, I am all a-shake.
At thirty I knew nothing! *'No!*
You must be joking! Thirty! Oh!'
I see, dear, you already know
the ins and outs of it. Heigh-ho!

Thus her father, on this rather
early fit of birds and bees:
how awful! (Azaïs, I think,
could classify his Mania).
Our little Inchbold, poor and pretty,
hurried now toward the city.
Jesus, Lord of Love, have pity!
She knows the ins and outs. Heigh-ho!

Hardly had she come to town
a Bishop took her well in hand
and Biblicly deodorized
she left her bed for higher things;
and, resolute, our little maid
her ecstasies to God repaid
and at His tender feet was laid.
She knows the ins and outs. Heigh-ho!

And now she has her Coat of Arms,
her riches and her pew in Church;
and dear Lord Roger, hot with wine,
has promised her a small chateau.
Thus our little protégé
trips on her merry, envied way
and to the King Himself might say,
She knows the ins and outs. Heigh-ho!

Thirst for Love

'Helen, I am utterly'
– Augustus MacKeat

Come quickly hither, pretty maid,
that on thy breast I may forget
my madness,
that through this darksome vale of sadness
follows at the pilgrim's back.

Some, seeking glory, spend their days
in bothered business, hour on hour:
but I
scornful of this earthly lie,
spend all upon my thirst for love!

Come quickly hither, pretty maid,
that on thy breast I may forget
my madness,
that through this darksome vale of sadness
follows at the pilgrim's back.

Some drink the overflowing cup
and live amongst the heady heights:
I yet,
my bitter nectar to forget,
spend all upon my thirst for love!

Come quickly hither, pretty maid,
that on thy breast I may forget
my madness,
that through this darksome vale of sadness
follows at the pilgrim's back.

Some steal and hoard, and pass their time
on treasure-chests in mean alarm:
I still,
without a treasury to fill,
spend all upon my thirst for love!

Come quickly hither, pretty maid,
that on thy breast I may forget
my madness,
that through this darksome vale of sadness
follows at the pilgrim's back.

The Englishman carves on his tomb
verses dreary as his days:
I too,
my lyre cast down amongst the rue,
spend all upon my thirst for love!

Come quickly hither, pretty maid,
that on thy breast I may forget
my madness,
that through this darksome vale of sadness
follows at the pilgrim's back.

And Time shall kill beneath its wings
the fire of all my fairest days
while I
wanting still to serve, and die,
spend all upon my thirst for love!

Come quickly hither, pretty maid,
that on thy breast I may forget
my madness,
that through this darksome vale of sadness
follows at the pilgrim's back.

A FIRE AT THE MARKETPLACE

'I live in the mountains, and Iove the vales'
– Le Victomte D'Arlincourt

I asked you to dance at Hazel-wood,
and there I danced with you:
and do you wear your white dress yet
for one you love, my sweet Jeanette?

Forsake me not for some rash cad,
some playhouse swank, dear Colombine,
there at the inn where first we met:
those flashing eyes that thrilled my heart
beneath the long, grey, windless sky!
O write if you wear your white dress yet
for one you love, my sweet Jeanette!

Fire! Fire! The breathless cry!
The Market burns! Oh, fire! Fire!
Is it Margot, Kate or Madeleine?…
No, no, it's Trooper Matthew's girl! –
O run my flower, run quickly now!
And tell me you saved your white dress yet
for one you love, my sweet Jeanette!

O more than the monster, Fire, beware
the strutting punk, the pedlar rude,
the handsome Guard with fancy hat,
for a maid is light as a windlestraw!
Run to Blois, and your lonely boy:
and bring with you your white dress yet
for one you love, my sweet Jeanette!

I asked you to dance at Hazel-wood,
and there I danced with you:
and do you wear your white dress yet
for one you love, my sweet Jeanette?

PATRIOTS

'We go to war against the nobility, guilty allies of the Bourbons, to
clear the way to the throne of Orleans. We perceive, at each step, the
efforts of this party to destroy the Court, its enemy, and yet allow that
royalty to remain. But the fall of the one will drag the other to its
destruction. No royalty may do without its patriarchy.'
– Louis de Saint-Just, the National Convention

'No more kicks up the arse!'
– The Rev. Duchesne

The Night of the 28ᵗʰ

'What is it, the death of a king, the fall of an empire? A clod, weighty
or no, that one throws in a grave'
– Gérard

'The great seem great to us only because we are on our knees'
– Eugène Scribe

I.

Moon, high witness of our splendours,
saw you ever from your Heaven
such a sacred night!
Looked upon such victory,
smiled on cities more sublime
with thy watchful light?

Never, ah, Segunto brave,
did Paris ever hurt so nobly,
reckon men so bold!
Men like shadows, flitting, silent,
digging 'midst the bloody storm
the universal grave!

No candle burns, no lighted door;
'tis darker than a forest deep,
and weary Paris sleeps.
But here and there your beams alight
upon a wall or jitty-stone
stained with heroes' gore:

or dabbles on a corse waylaid,
its skull half-cracked, with gaping eye,
lumped naked 'cross the stones;
the infamous in banners wrapped,
borne on spits of bloodied swords
in bloody, bold parade!

And sometimes, in this crouchèd night,
the ring of axes, clash of blades,
the rattle-clattered spear,
the shouts of guards, the Who-Goes-There,
a rebel crashing somewhere o'er
the shattered helms in flight.

And sometimes muskets, cannons, shells,
cracks and thunders, whistled shots
that rip the screaming air
and cries of Death! Beware! Alarm!
and tears and curses, calls to arms
that jangle 'midst the bells.

II.
The greybeard here, the shepherd there,
the beaten child, the girl, the friends,
the rich, the ragged, all as one:
Hope lights upon the barricades!
Whilst at the doors the Myrmidons
defend the mansions locked and barred,
each house, each chair an armoury,
each gate, each wall a powder keg,
each darkling roof a sheet of shot!

And Paris burns with prayers and steel
all offered up in mad dismay
amidst the very flames of Hell!

III.
Here sits a maiden, fond with love,
who ties a ribbon in her hair
and waits her love's return;
and hears his footsteps on the stair,
and smiles that there is Peace at last,
while on the street his body burns.

IV.
What is this fallen, darksome thing
that echoes to the moonlit storm?
This house despoiled of lights and lackeys,
empty couches, loveless beds?
Where the Watch, the loud alarm?
It is the palace of the King.

Old, debauched and desecrate,
he flees in terror to Saint-Cloud,
and there this little Nero lies
truckled on his terraces
and peeps upon his butchers' work –
the slaughter of his baffled State.

Enjoy your handiwork! Your sweet
revenge, your fireworks, your feast!
For nothing lacks to entertain.
Enjoy the desperate mothers' screams
that call their sons in frantic wise
whilst they are felled like fields of wheat.

The night is done, and dawn is near,
so quick, ye dogs, lickspittles, rats,
bring forth your hunting horns, your hounds –
the Devil wants more blood! Come now,
bring forth your bloody flaying-blades
and lap the blood that gushes here!

v.
And still the People cannot know
what chance may hap, what end will come;
what struggles in the womb of time,
what victory, what dark dismay;
but, bound to Liberty, they rise
to fight once more, and scorn their fate.

Here Lafayette, a Brutus brave,
cries 'France!' – his fevered, stricken call
from out his weltered sickbed rings.
He brandishes his sword on high
and falls afaint amidst the dawn.
The sun is up! It shines anew
before his eyes – red, white, and blue!

ON THE WOUNDS OF THE INSTITUTE

And is it true, ye French? Can it be true
you let some vile despoiler's hand
in rash affront obscure the scars
you bear upon your brow like stars?

And is it true, July, that envious men
are hateful of your noble mien,
your heart's-blood gushed from out your veins?
Foul splatterers! New featherbrains!

Zounds!
Render now the honour due to heroes' wounds!

TO THE COURT THAT PROPOSED THE ABOLITION OF THE DEATH PENALTY

'Well then, be unbending: it is indulgence that is ferocious, because it threatens our country'
– Louis de Saint-Just

In vain the murderer seeks to fly the axe,
the bright, avenging, executioner's fire:
this stain no ocean washes from his hands:
the blade is still withdrawen from its sheath
and shall not e'er return from where it struck,
and pierced its victim's side and bathed the more
in his quick blood, that corridor to make
out which Revenge shall wake!

In vain, when God and Man do all approve
the blame, and brand him with his sin for aye;
to seek some limit to the punishment
and thrust its righteous instruments away.
Live by the sword; die by the sword – our God
proclaimed it in the mercy of his grace.
Blood is spilt: 'tis right that all men cry
that Cain must surely die.

So, what mistitled folly, Sire, was yours
when first you pleaded thus your vicious hope,
poor coward of a Governance denied,
that was the mindless favour of a King?
In vain you seek to dress your insolence
in funeral weeds, and strut the common stage –
but, ah! the common man you misconstrue
has keener eyes than you!

Your bounty made to fit your circumstance,
your timely-tendered melter of our hearts!
Ah, truly, I am honoured by thee, Sire,
and much obliged for your kind obligation!
I humbly beg your leave. I owe it you,
dear Gentleman. 'Tis true! You know us well,
and all we here, mere numbskulls in this case.
Oh pardon, we are base.

These Lords shall never be condemned to die;
their heads stand still above the common law!
Their deeds, if ours the plots and crimes of death,
are *exploits* for the merry Gentlemen.
Ah, toothless Tribunes would ye be if they
all trembled not, and thought your mercy light.
It seems the axeman executes the law
only on the poor.

Unfortunate! What has he done? In poverty
he dared to counterfeit a little coin.
The Judge jumps for his cap of Death – 'tis done!
So quickly has this beggar lived... and died.
Yet he who over-smirches still the world
and plagues the nation with his rotted sin,
whose sword is drawn for perjury and strife
would have the beggar's life!

It cannot be. Ah, Man, lift up your eyes
in unecclesiastic wise. See now
this castle, filled with History's brave souls,
their swords and banners dripping in their hands,
a bloody sceptre twixt their furious teeth,
and calling on the law of Eye for Eye,
as lions, turning from their fallen prey,
roar loud at bay.

'Tis Berton! Little man of fierce success,
a noble heart who fell into disgrace;
'tis Sergeants Four, the Knights of La Rochelle;
the luckless Caron, proud Labédayère,
spiked with shot upon the wide Grenelle;
The Mowers bold, and Mouton-Duvernay;
and Marshall Ney, the thunderbolt of war –
and a thousand more!
The bloody sacrifice of Saint-Denis,
all, all, the trampled heroes of our time.
Alas, our axes fell not swift and sure
to vengeance! Martyrs! May your names be blessed,
and more, who on their brows have crowns of gold
that came in Death's insatiable hand:
Farcy and Arcole, the last to die,
the heroes of July.

'Tis only they who might the balance take
of Justice, and absolve their killers cruel.
But Death has stilled their hands: and in that hush
you fabricate your pitiable plans!
But when they fell they cried for vengeance still:
did you not hear them shout, my friend? Ah, well,
a little less of grovelling mercy then.
He dies. Amen.

Our suffering does not oppress *your* hearts,
that scuttled, panic-struck, at Corsic's news:
down on your knees – your Emperor returns –
and weep repentance at his feet, ye Sires,
who nothing lost, no friend, no lovers dear,
who care not what our greatest men have done.
So, weep before the guillotine in vain –
let Holyrood complain.

REVEILLE SONG

'Advance, my company!
My heroes – like The Cid!'
– Riego's Anthem

The desperate spur is blooded on our sides
beneath the Royal heel – but now, my friends,
the rider free has trampled underfoot
the heady circlet of the fallen King,
and smashes from its hinge the flound'ring gate
that slaven swords and hands have shored in vain;
and barely has he broke to Freedom's fray
than others seize the reins and ride away!

On, on, my men, more terrible! more bold
than Roland and Bayard!
Ye shall be free, ye shall be kings, ye slaves!
On, on, my men! On, on!

We know what strength lies in our hearts, we know
three days are all it takes to fell a King;
too happy then, we slumbered in our tents,
the iron sceptres heavy on our dreams,
and, ah! too soon we left the battlefield,
resheathed our swords, and gave the field away.
Already Freedom other paths doth take,
weeping in our names: Frenchmen! Awake!

On, on, my men, more terrible! more bold
than Roland and Bayard!
Ye shall be free, ye shall be kings, ye slaves!
On, on, my men! On, on!

Our enemy has ta'en the Antique Man
in nets, and lays false kisses on his brow,
and hides in cloaks and mantles of Free Men
to walk amongst us safe and strait. Oh, France!
let us reclaim our honoured Guide, strike down
the fawning priests who smile and plot! And know,
the man who is not with us is our foe!

On, on, my men, more terrible! more bold
than Roland and Bayard!
Ye shall be free, ye shall be kings, ye slaves!
On, on, my men! On, on!

Our bloody cries awake the Belgic hearts;
and Belgic freedom echoes to the skies;
and Kosciusko rises! How now goes
Old Poland? Ha! 'Tis shot in one fell night!
Two tyrants have mislaid their slavish fee!
And to these new-found lands I cry *Well done!*
Our bourgeois King sits trembling in his cloak:
whilst tyrants howl, the earth throws off its yoke!

On, on, my men, more terrible! more bold
than Roland and Bayard!
Ye shall be free, ye shall be kings, ye slaves!
On, on, my men! On, on!

And do we shatter now our servitude
to bow to some new gold? What butcher now
doth knead our hearts and minds with old deceits,
our swords set down, our suffering renewed?
Arise! and on our marble backs shall stand
the statue of some perfect Liberty!
The people gather round in Freedom's sight
and cry to Heav'n – and rise into the light!

On, on, my men, more terrible! more bold
than Roland and Bayard!
Ye shall be free, ye shall be kings, ye slaves!
On, on, my men! On, on!

AFTERWORD

to P. Avril, Secretary of The Friends of the People

> *'The Aristocrat says he will destroy himself;*
> *but he lies, heart and soul;*
> *he will destroy us, and knows it well'*
> – Louis de Saint-Just

How feeble are ye, weak and servile men;
how feeble, though the world may think you fair;
how feeble and how vile your spotted souls,
ye Royal carrion, vultures of the air!

How feeble are ye, compost, sludge and sewer;
ye farted yeast that bursts in blistered reek;
your slavish lips immured in mud and lies
cry 'Bravo, Sire!' and poison as they speak.

The Devil! ye deserve your tyrants vile,
that crack their whips and starve your hearts with shit;
ye grocers, drunk with pow'r at one free shot,
ye winders of the King's flesh-laden spit.

And he that tells ye Kings are made in Hell,
that Lords are festered scabs, and Men are free,
ye call an Anarchist, and Born to Hang,
and make a scaffold out of ev'ry tree.

A fool ye are! Be still. Who wants your life?
Ye pitiful and proud, ye weather-cock!
Your neck is saved, unless the headsman's axe
mislays, and falls beneath the chopping-block!

EPILOGUE

'Listen! Listen! Listen!'
– Bürger

''Twas Hunger laid Malfilâtre low'
– Gilbert

You think me happy, *nice, correct* and *calm,*
because I smile and smile and do no harm,
because I live without Ambition's care,
without regrets, a virgin to despair;
but see you not, within my wallèd breast,
the parchment heart, the fire dispossessed!
A shaded lamp is duller to the sight;
it must, like hearts, be broken for its light.

Poor André! When your head drew near the blade
you raged upon the tumbril, ah! dismayed
that you must leave your country still undone,
its glory and its freedom yet unwon.
And I, in the extremity of need,
rage too! I strike the rocks of life! I bleed!
I cry to Heav'n how I am tortured still,
who feels his power, yet bears a shackled will.

Power!… irons!… ha, no. A Poet, mum,
who tries for Heaven but whose muse is dumb.
Strength lies in chains. Away! For who may bear
this gaudy time, bereft of Good. Beware!
and Work: for who believes that better waits?
Work! for howling Destitution baits
each thought that comes like hope in solitude.
What says my lute in answer? – only *Food!*